The Yoga of Radiant Presence

revealed in

The Gospel of Thomas

The YOGA of RADIANT PRESENCE

revealed in

THE GOSPEL OF THOMAS

PETER BROWN

THE OPEN DOORWAY

2020

© 2020 PETER BROWN

INTRODUCTION

The Gospel of Thomas is one of the many apocryphal gospels that were in circulation in the first few centuries of Christianity. It was discovered near Nag Hammadi, Egypt, in 1945. It dates from the very early years of Christianity, written in perhaps AD 60-140.

It consists of 114 sayings attributed to Jesus. These are remarkable from a spiritual perspective, in that unlike many sayings of Jesus from other gospels, which convey perhaps more vague spirituality or moral teachings, many of these sayings give very specific instructions in realizing the true nature of this reality.

These instructions, rightly understood, align perfectly with the highest Yoga teachings of all traditions. The Yoga of Radiant Presence is a name that has been given to this comprehensive Yoga, distilled into its essence purified from the accidental historical, traditional, and philosophical differences of these established traditions.

Here are presented selected sayings from the Gospel that most clearly convey this Yoga, with explanations of their meaning and nuance. The intention of this presentation is to make these teachings practically available to modern yogis, without the need to become immersed into Christian tradition or the intricacies of different historical Yogic traditions.

The sayings that were omitted here are generally moralistic, more obscure parables, or lessons that do not directly teach the Yoga of Radiant Presence.

These sayings have been retranslated from the original Coptic of the Nag Hammadi scroll.

RADIANT PRESENCE

The teachings of Jesus in the Gospel of Thomas are about the nature of human reality and were Jesus' instructions to his disciples, teaching how to see and understand what it truly is for themselves.

Human reality is entirely the miraculous presence of the experiential field. This is a self-evident, infinite, inclusive continuum, which constitutes all of reality. Anything whatsoever that is held to exist is actually an apparition within this.

This field is not what it may be generally held to be within human understanding. It is miraculously present, atemporal (instantaneous with no past, future, or duration), and aspatial (omnipresent and absolutely inclusive).

This field is entirely full of apparent patterning of infinitely differentiated experiential qualities, for example color, sound, taste, thought, and infinite other unnameable specifics. These apparent characteristics are infinite in their quantity and differentiation.

The apparent patterning that appears cannot be resolved to actually exist in any precise configuration, due to its infinity of information and absolute instantaneous dynamism. So since no particular pattern can be precisely resolved, the Radiance, even though seeming to be apparently patterned, is paradoxically actually unpatterned.

There is present an intelligent functionality that spontaneously analyzes the apparent patterning and creates ideas of specific stable coherent patterns within the field, by using imaginary averaging and censorship of experiential detail. These patterns can then be imagined to be coherent entities, objects, conditions, bodies, worlds, etc. In fact, any such patterns are actually nothing other than the infinitely dynamic, unpatterned Radiance, and no such coherent entities, objects, conditions, bodies, worlds, etc. can be found to actually exist at all.

Thus a "consensus reality" can seem to exist, consisting of an objectively existing material world inhabited by oneself in one's body, in complex interrelation with other objects and beings; but in actuality, only the experiential field exists. All these worlds, bodies, things, situations, etc. are abstracted in imagination from direct experience of the unresolvable field, which alone is actual.

These elaborate interpretational frameworks exist in imagination only. All the details of what seems to constitute one's human situation are pure fantasy; all that actually exists is the fundamentally unresolvable, hence uninterpretable, infinite field of the Radiance.

This worldview is not a theory, but a self-evident, undeniable, pragmatic fact, clearly verified by careful examination of one's experience. Any other worldview depends upon hypothetical assumption and imaginary abstraction, i.e., fantasy.

The experiential field can be called Radiant Presence, after the two most prominent aspects of its nature: its miraculous Presence/Being, existing spontaneously and eternally, depending upon nothing; and its Radiance, the fact that it constantly spontaneously radiates an infinite differentiation of apparent experiential characteristics with absolute instantaneous dynamism.

YOGA

Yoga is a traditional name for the process of investigating one's reality to discover its actual nature, and a yogi is one who undertakes this investigation. The Yoga of Radiant Presence is the investigation of Radiant Presence (experience) by Radiant Presence (consciousness) to discover Radiant Presence (this entire system of reality).

Through Yoga, the yogi discovers the true condition that their defined self, body, and world actually consists of: the ultimately unpatterned miracle of the field of Radiant Presence. This does not necessarily negate the mental perspective of the defined self and world, which may continue to be experienced as a mental perspective within the actual, known, solely existing field of Radiant Presence; but the yogi will clearly and certainly know that the infinite unresolvable field alone exists, and that their familiar, defined perspective is merely an arbitrary way of imagining it to be.

This view of human reality is what is being presented within the Gospel of Thomas, as will be demonstrated below. Jesus (or the author of this Gospel if in fact other than the historic Jesus), as revealed by this Gospel, was a teacher of Radiant Presence, directly pointing out this condition to his disciples.

TERMINOLOGY OF THE GOSPEL

In many of the sayings, the disciples are seeking the *Kingdom*. This refers to the field of Radiant Presence. *Entering the Kingdom* means coming to know the actuality of this reality as it truly is.

The *Father* refers to the causal nature of Radiant Presence, the fact that the inherent nature of Radiant Presence itself is the cause of everything and anything that seems to exist. All differentiation/apparent patterning of the field occurs solely due to the inherent nature of the Radiant Presence, so it itself is the cause of anything that is being interpreted as phenomena.

The *Kingdom of the Father* is the field of Radiant Presence and its all-powerful nature.

Several times in these sayings the disciples are told they can become *sons of the Father*. *Sons of the Father* or *son of Man* (son of Adam elsewhere in biblical language) refers to the presence of a seemingly embodied human self experientially existing within the known true context of Radiant Presence. *Son of Adam* implies this same direct interrelationship with the Father since Adam, directly created by God, is manifestly the presence of God.

(This point of the coexistence of a relatively coherent human perspective within the subsuming actuality of the infinite Radiance, and the mystery that these seemingly divergent perspectives can both be present in one's experience without contradiction, is central to the experience of yogic realization.)

In these sayings *life* or *living* refers to the absolute dynamism of the Radiance. All action, all change, all of the ceaseless movement of everything in experience is the very nature of the Radiance and is the sole liveliness, or life: there is no life other than this.

Dead refers to static entities imagined to exist stably, persistently, and objectively, such as bodies, things, or the world. These stable, autonomously existing things, beings, bodies, etc. exist only in imagination. In actuality there is nothing whatsoever but the pure dynamism of the infinite unresolvable apparent patterning of the Radiance, the *life*.

Light versus *darkness* likewise refers to the known certainty of the actuality of the Radiance versus the ignorance of imagined static, relatively inert beings, bodies, and things. *Light* is the direct textural experience of the Presence of Radiance; darkness by contrast is the lack of acknowledging this light-like quality of experience itself.

THE GOSPEL OF THOMAS

These are the hidden words which Jesus, who is life, spoke, and which Didymos Judas Thomas wrote down.

This introduction identifies Jesus as being Life. Life is actually the being of the field of reality, the experiential field, the Radiant Presence which alone exists. So by identifying Jesus as being this field, he is revealed by implication to be beyond the erroneous identification with existing as a separate dependent human being, and to be a realized being, one who realizes their true condition. He is therefore nothing other than the transcendental field of Radiant Presence, and hence empowered to teach this true perspective.

(1) And he said,

"Whoever discovers the meaning of these words will not taste death."

One of the essential aspects of the Radiant Presence is that it exists as the solely existent eternal now and extraspatial here, and does not consist of or contain separate persistent beings or entities that either begin or cease.

The seeker who comes to understand the perspective being taught in these words will come to see that they do not exist as a separate entity that can cease to be, but rather that they are nothing other than the eternal Radiance itself. Their previous misidentification to be existing as such an entity will be invalidated. Knowing themselves to be eternal being not subject to cessation, they will not "taste death."

Another aspect of this means that knowing the meaning of these teachings, knowing the actual living Presence of the Radiance, they will know and experience that all apparent things and conditions are intrinsically nothing other than this living Presence itself; so, there is nothing dead or inert to be experienced, there is no "death" to be "tasted."

(2) Jesus said this:
"Let one who seeks not stop seeking until he finds.
When he finds, he will be troubled.
After he is troubled he will be amazed,
and he will discover that he is king over All."

Here the yogi is encouraged to persist in Yoga until some realization of the actual condition occurs. When this happens they will be "troubled" by the discovery of how radically different their actual condition is from what they had previously held it to be. The initial disorientation of trying to adjust to the implications of this new condition can be profound, even shocking.

As the initial disorientation due to the contrast between the newly revealed condition and the previously held inaccurate conception dies down, and the Yogi relaxes into orienting to their actual condition, they will begin to be "amazed" as they come to appreciate and enjoy the astounding nature of the actuality they will have discovered.

One aspect of this nature is that the yogi is in actuality nothing other than the field of Radiant Presence itself, which is the agent of its own functioning. Thus it is ruling ("king") "over" itself, which is "All"; so the yogi discovers themself to be entirely this actual omnipotence ("king over All").

(3) Jesus said,
"If those who lead you say to you, 'See, the Kingdom is in the sky,'
then the birds of the sky will have priority above you.
If they say to you, 'It is in the sea,' then the fish will precede you.
Rather, the Kingdom is inside of you, and it is outside of you.
When you come to know what you are,
then you will become realized,
and you will know that you are the sons of the living Father.
However if you will not know yourselves, it
will seem that you exist in poverty and that you are that poverty."

The first two sentences of this saying caution against seeking the true condition of Radiant Presence (the "Kingdom") in any literally spatial perceptual portion of the experience of the yogi, in the seemingly external environment that the unrealized perspective holds to be one's situation. In other words, it is not a material thing or location.

Then Jesus points out that it actually exists both subjectively and objectively ("is inside you, and it is outside you"), so it thus exists in all portions of the experiential field rather than only in the seemingly "external" objective space.

Then he says that when you realize what you are, what the "Kingdom" is, you realize yourself, the human being and persona that you have identified yourself as being, to be a subsystem of the Radiant Presence, "sons of the living Father."

But if this is not known, then the absolute meaningfulness and fullness of the actual condition will not be appreciated, and the normal human interpretation of your environment and yourself that seems to be true will have a relative quality of poverty ("it will seem that you exist in poverty and you are that poverty"), by contrast with the profound richness that it actually is.

(5) Jesus said this:
"Know what is in front of your face,
and what is hidden will be revealed to you.
For there is nothing hidden that will not appear to investigation."

This saying points out that the actual condition of Radiant Presence can be discovered in the normal present experience of the yogi, that which is "in front of your face."

"What is hidden" is the actual condition of the yogi, the inclusive being of Radiant Presence, which is "hidden" by the materialist misinterpretations of consensus reality. So by investigating (coming to "know") his present experience he can discover this true condition ("what is hidden will be revealed to you").

The last line points out the insubstantiality of these misconceptions, that can be easily invalidated by intelligent investigation of the obvious Radiant qualities of the actual Presence of experience.

**(6)   His disciples questioned him and said to him,
"Do you want us to fast? How should we pray?
Should we give alms? What diet shall we follow?"
Jesus said, "Do not tell lies, and do not do what you hate,
for all things are revealed in the presence of heaven.
Nothing you think hidden is not actually apparent,
and nothing you think covered is actually concealed."**

The disciples inquire how they should behave, with the implication that if they behave some certain way it will be advantageous for them in discovering the true condition.

Jesus' advice is to be truthful, and to behave as they truly want to; in other words, to be honestly what they are, and not to try to be what they are not.

"All things are revealed in the presence of heaven" means that "all things" are no more than Radiance revealed in the Presence, regardless of what they seem to be in interpretation; so contrivance is fruitless. Any change in superficial behavior would be fundamentally no more than just Radiance, just as it was prior to the change, so nothing can be achieved.

(As the goal of realizing the true condition is to realize Radiant Presence just as it is, there is no advantage in trying to change superficial appearances. For example, if you could change what was happening in a dream, it would still be only dreaming, just as it was before the change.)

All the nuance of meanings and flavors of experience are explicit ("nothing you think hidden is not apparent"); the patternings of the Radiance are clear and available to observation, so strategies of subterfuge conceal nothing (Nothing you think hidden is not actually apparent, and nothing you think covered is actually concealed").

(7) Jesus said,
"The lion is blessed which the man eats,
and the lion becomes man;
and cursed is the man whom the lion eats,
and the lion will become man."

The "lion" symbolizes the crude animal nature of the ignorant persona identified with misinterpretations of their nature and circumstance, caught up in emotional behavior reactive to the imagined conditions of their misinterpretation.

The "man" here symbolizes a perspective above the animal perspective, in this case the lucid intelligence that clearly apprehends the true condition, Radiant Presence.

If the man eats the lion, then the ignorant partialized perspective is subsumed into the true perspective (the "man"), and "the lion becomes man." The partialized perspective is integrated into the context of the true being of Radiant Presence. Thus the "lion" (the ignorant perspective of the immature yogi) becomes blessed by having their perspective released into its true condition.

But if the lion eats the man, then the true perspective ("man") is subsumed into the misunderstanding of ignorance (the "lion") and becomes lost in interpretation and dominated by needless reactivity and emotion ("the lion becomes man"). Thus the truth of the "man" (the realized perspective of Radiant Presence) becomes hidden within misinterpretation and emotional reactivity, thus becomes "cursed."

(11) Jesus said,
"This heaven will pass away, and the one above it will pass away, and the dead do not live, and the living will not die.
In the days when you ate what is dead, you made it alive.
When you come to be in the light, what will you do?
On the day when you were one, you were made of the two; but when you become two, what will you do?"

The "heavens will pass away" refers to the passing of all apparent perspectives as they transition into some other perspective. The waking world yields to sleep, sleep yields to dream, the world of life yields to death, morning yields to afternoon, this moment yields to the "next," and so on. All of these perspectives, no more than ghostly "heavens," are apparent configurations of the patternings of the Radiance, which eternally morph and move into newness.

"The dead do not live, and the living will not die"—The "dead," which are apparitions (objects and entities that are imaginatively held to exist autonomously in experience), "do not live" but are mere fantasies, side effects, of what is actual (Radiant Presence), whose nature is what "lives." Experience, experiencing itself, is what actually exists, is alive, is life. Experience never actually becomes the apparent objects of experience, even though it enables "them" to appear. It will never cease nor become inanimate, hence it "will not die."

Making the dead alive by "eating" (experiencing) it means that the patterns being experienced explicitly become experience, life itself, and "dead" objects are thereby revealed to not exist as anything static. So the very fact of experiencing the patterns reveals that they are not autonomous, but are known to be experience itself, actual life itself. They are transformed from mere "dead" supposed objects into "alive," dynamic Radiant experience.

When the yogi "comes into the light," comes to know the Radiant Presence, there is seen to be no separate objective world, no separate engagement of a subject with objects, so "the dead" will no longer be "eaten." In this koan-like question ("what will you do?"), in this actionless, objectless, transcendental actuality, what then is actually being done?

"The day when you were one" refers to the sole actual Presence, which includes and is "made of," the "two" (both apparent subjectivity and objectivity); yet it is actually nothing other than the inclusive experiential continuum of Radiant Presence ("one"). But if the subject and the objective environment were each held to be actually separate, "become two," what then? The only recourse would be Yoga.

(15) Jesus said,
"When you should look upon one who was not born of woman,
prostrate yourselves on your faces and worship him.
What is there is your Father."

"One who was not born of woman" refers to something existing without prior process, not coming into existence as a result of apparent cause and effect processes of preexisting conditions. Its being is not dependent on anything separate.

Radiant Presence exists miraculously, instantaneously, and does not come from or depend upon something else; it shines forth only from itself in and as the instant.

This then is "the Father," the true being of the Radiant Presence, origin, and creator of "everything." So when the yogi recognizes the miraculous instantaneous Presence of experience, Jesus is pointing out that this includes and creates all, and is the supreme being, hence worthy of being worshiped.

(17) Jesus said,

"I shall give you what an eye has not seen and what an ear has not heard and what a hand has not touched and what has never occurred to the human mind."

Radiant Presence cannot be seen, heard, felt, or conceived of as it truly is, even though what IS seen, heard, and felt is nothing other than the Radiance; but its nature is vastly beyond the implications of cursorily interpreted sensory information. Likewise thought is nothing other than the Radiance, but the content of thought is incapable of accurately reflecting the actual nature of Radiant Presence.

It is only in the recognition of its inherent infinity that experience is known for what it truly is, which demands sensitive, intimate, intelligent examination, Yoga, to be discovered. Jesus says that he gives the disciples this perspective, here in these teachings.

> **(18) The disciples said to Jesus,**
> **"Tell us in what way our end will be."**
> **Jesus said,**
> **"Have you discovered the beginning, that you look for the end?**
> **For in the place the beginning is, there will the end be.**
> **Blessed is he who will be standing in the beginning;**
> **he will know the end and will not taste death."**

The question of the disciples reflects the consensus reality belief that they exist as separate beings who will have an end. Jesus points out that they have never actually found their beginning, so the assumption of an end is supposition only.

"The place the beginning is, there will the end be" means the beginning and the end are in actuality this single instantaneous present existing beyond space and time, always here and always now. All apparent beginnings and endings are in fact nothing other than this timeless Presence alone.

"He who will be standing in the beginning" is the fully realized consciousness of actuality that is, and clearly knows, the true condition, the "beginning." He therefore also "know(s) the end," this eternal endless being, which has no cessation; therefore the yogi will not "taste death."

(22) **Jesus saw infants suckling.
He said to his disciples,
"These infants being suckled are like those
who enter the Kingdom."
They said to him, "Then, if we become children,
we will enter the Kingdom?"
Jesus said this to them:**
"When you make the two one, and when you make the inside
like the outside and the outside like the inside,
and what is above like what is below,
and when you make the male and the woman one and the same,
so that the male not become male nor the woman become woman;
and when you make eyes instead of an eye,
and a hand instead of a hand, and a foot instead of a foot,
and an image instead of an image;
then will you enter the Kingdom."

———————

The infants being suckled are being completely nourished and protected. Likewise, the yogi who realizes Radiant Presence ("enter[s] the Kingdom") discovers that all that they are and all that they know is provided by, sustained by, and supported by the natural condition of the Radiance, like the children.

The disciples then suppose they need to become children to know the true situation (the "Kingdom"). Jesus then explains what they must actually realize:

Making the two one means seeing that all division is nonexistent. There is only the one Radiance, and all separate things or entities are imagined.

Inside and outside refer to subjectivity and objectivity: these are nothing other than the one experience. The division into subjective and objective is in mental interpretation only.

Above and below refer to degrees of coarseness/fineness of experience, "below" being more coarse material qualities and "above" being more subtle qualities of thought and psychic nuances, which likewise come to be known as actually degrees of the same thing.

Male and female refer to active and passive, doer and the conditions acted upon. So making these "one and the same" is knowing that the true being of the Radiance functions spontaneously without partialization into doer and done, cause and effect.

"Eyes instead of an eye, and a hand instead of a hand, and a foot instead of a foot, and an image instead of an image" means that the "objects" eye, hand, and foot are actually no more than ideas of these things superimposed within uninterpretable experience. The first reference to the thing refers to the actual uninterpretable Radiance being experienced, the experiential actuality that is being designated as that thing. The second is the concept of that as a "thing." So Jesus says that when you orient to the experiential textural actuality that is being called eye, hand, and foot instead of the belief that those "things" actually exist as the static, objective objects that the concepts define them to be (the second "eye," "hand," and "foot"), then you will "enter the Kingdom"— realize all of reality to be Radiant Presence.

Likewise the "image" (interpretation, the second use of "image") of what things, entities, and circumstances seem to be is merely conceptual. This must be replaced by the knowledge that actual imagination (the first "image"), the presence of which enables the holding of these conceptual definitions, is itself actually the Presence of Radiance entirely. ("An image [the presence of the actuality of imagination] instead of an image" [the interpretation that is imagined to exist]).

Once these misunderstandings are seen through, then one "enters the Kingdom," i.e., knows their true condition to be nothing other than this transcendental Radiant Presence.

**(24) His disciples said,
"Show us the place where you are,
because it is necessary for us to seek after it."
He said to them, "He who has an ear, let him listen.
There is light within a man of light,
and he becomes light to the whole world.
If he does not become light, he is darkness."**

The disciples wonder where, in what condition, Jesus exists.

"He who has an ear" refers to the actual experiencer, the perceptual intelligence of Radiant Presence itself (which alone experiences, has the ability to hear ["has an ear"], and has the ability to understand the perspective Jesus is communicating due to recognizing this as its own inherent perspective). So Jesus is inviting the perceiving intelligence (rather than the conceptualizing mind), which alone has the ability to understand the truth that he is saying, to listen to his teaching.

The "light within a man of light" is the knowledge of the true condition ("light") that is possessed by ("within") a "man of light," one who clearly knows themselves to be this condition, the Radiant Presence. He then "becomes light to the whole world"— he displays his knowledge in his words and actions, which can be perceived by anyone with sensitivity.

But if the yogi does not realize the Radiance, does not "become light," they will identify themself to be what is untrue, "is darkness."

(27) Jesus said,
"If you don't fast from the world, you will not find the Kingdom.
If you do not hold what is sacred to be sacred,
you will not see the Father."

To "fast from the world" means to refrain from orienting to one's experience and one's functioning in accordance with materialistic, consensus-reality interpretations about what one is and what one's world is, and what their interrelation is. He says this is required to "find the Kingdom," to recognize the reality of Radiant Presence.

To know what is sacred, to appreciate the absolute nature of Radiant Presence as it is and to recognize its miraculous nature ("hold what is sacred to be sacred"): this is necessary to "see the Father," to clearly know the source and essence of reality.

> **(28) Jesus said,**
> **"I stood up in the midst of the world,**
> **and I appeared to them in flesh.**
> **I found all of them drunk; I found none of them thirsting.**
> **And my soul felt pain for the sons of men,**
> **because they are blind in their minds and do not recognize reality;**
> **for they came to the world empty,**
> **and they will also leave the world empty.**
> **But now they are drunk;**
> **when their wine wears off, then they will repent."**

Here Jesus laments that the majority of people are "drunk" on their delusions and "blind in their minds," believing in their inaccurate consensus reality interpretations of themselves and their situation; not recognizing the reality as it actually is, nor realizing that they are missing the true situation, so not "thirsting" for it.

That they came into the world "empty" and will leave it so refers to a newborn's arrival into worldly experience in a perfectly open, direct, uninterpreted state: and likewise upon death the interpretations of oneself, one's body and worldly life disappear in the loss of bodily experience.

This line also can refer to the fact that falling into believing in a "world" that one inhabits occurs within (and never becomes other than) the uninterpretable Radiance, which is not a world or anything else, so is "empty"; and when those beliefs are seen through, "leav(ing) the world," this "emptiness" is all that remains.

But they are currently lost in imaginary interpretations of their being. When the interpretation is finally seen through, they will regret ("will repent") that they did not avail themselves of the wonderful richness, meaningfulness, and sacredness that the knowledge of their true condition would have afforded.

**(29) Jesus said,
"If the flesh came into being because of spirit, it is a wonder.
But if spirit came into being because of the body,
it would be a greater wonder.
But I am amazed at this,
how this great richness was placed in this poverty."**

That form, matter, appears due to the nature of Radiant Presence is a wonder, is an unexplainable miracle.

But if Radiant Presence came into existence from inert matter, it would be even stranger, as how could the dynamism, consciousness, and transcendental nature of the Radiance come from dead, inert form? How could the transcendental condition of consciousness be a mere byproduct of accidental combinations of inert matter?

Then Jesus comments how amazing it is that the transcendental nature and "great richness" of Radiant Presence exists in the apparent context of the difficulty and inelegance of seeming normal human life ("this poverty"), as most people imagine their lives to be.

(36) Jesus said,

"Do not be concerned from morning until evening and from evening until morning about what you will wear."

Here the yogi is admonished not to spend all their time concerning themself with worldly conditions ("what you will wear"), but rather (by implication) to seek and find the Radiance, the inherent condition that obtains, regardless of what superficial conditions are held to be.

**(37) His disciples said,
"When will you become revealed to us
and when shall we see you?"
Jesus said,
"When you strip yourselves naked without being ashamed
and take up your garments
and place them under your feet like little children
and trample them, then will you see the son of the living one,
and you will not be afraid."**

The disciples ask what conditions will obtain ("when") that will enable them to realize the condition of the Christ.

He directs them to "strip yourselves naked," which means to orient to themselves solely as being their experiencing, distinct from forms and interpreted things and situations they feel themselves to be "clothed" in.

"Without being ashamed" means not identifying with or relating emotionally to the forms and situations that they are accustomed to orienting to; fully releasing their identification with those orientations.

"Place them (their garments) under your feet like little children and trample them" means to then orient to the forms and apparent "things" in their experience innocently, carelessly, and with abandon. Then they will know ("see") the true condition of themselves to be virtual subsystems of inclusive Radiant Presence (the "son of the living one").

They will "not be afraid" because they will be freed from all imaginary dependency upon conditions needing to be any particular way for their safety, and from the attendant fear that those conditions might not be that way.

(50) Jesus said,
"If they say to you, 'Where are you from?' say this to them:
'We have come out of the light,
the place where the light shines out by its own nature
and stabilized itself and appeared forth in these images.'
If they say to you, 'Are you the light?' say this;
'We are its children, we are the chosen of the living Father.'
If they ask you, 'What is the sign of your Father in you?'
say to them, 'It is movement with repose.'"

This saying very fully states the perspective of Radiant Presence.

"We have come out of the light" means that all apparitions are abstracted by inherent intelligence from the infinite differentiation of the Radiance within itself, the apparitions of the disciples in this case.

The "place"— Presence is the sole "location"; "where the light shines out by its own nature"— the Radiance of the infinity of experiential qualities and textures shines forth solely due to the inherent nature of Radiant Presence; "and stabilized itself"— and presents with infinite information density enabling the apparition of seemingly coherent patterning; "and appeared forth in these images"— which is then abstracted by the inherent intelligence into the "images" of apparent things, entities, and situations.

"We are its children, we are the chosen of the living Father" means that as apparent entities they are "children" of the Radiance (as all apparent entities are "born out of" the Radiance by interpretation); and being chosen means that they are in alignment with the Radiant Presence, the "living Father," due to their knowing the actual condition and hence knowing their unity with, and place within, it.

The "sign of the Father" is "movement" (Radiance) "with repose" (Presence). The "sign of the Father" is "in (them)," as their knowing of and conscious alignment with this "movement with repose," the Radiant Presence.

**(51) His disciples said to him,
"Which day is the repose of the dead coming,
and when will the new world come?"
He said this to them,
"What you are looking out for has already come,
but you recognize it not."**

Here Jesus points out that the "new world," "what you are looking for," the Kingdom of heaven (Radiant Presence) "has already come," i.e., is already what this is. And "the repose of the dead" is already the case, as all forms already rest in their actual nature as Radiance, being "dead" in that forms have no life or animation in themselves, but are merely interpretations of the actual Radiance, which is the life, liveliness.

That they "recognize it not" is the sole issue that Yoga addresses.

The transcendent, sacred, absolute condition of Radiant Presence is all that has ever existed, but due to misinterpretation in imagination, belief, and emotional investment, the majority of humans do not recognize that this is the case and suffer with the difficult implications of their fantasies, held to be objectively true.

> **(52)   His disciples said to him,**
> **"Twenty-four prophets spoke in Israel,**
> **and all of them spoke in you."**
> **"You have left out the living one in your presence and have spoken about the dead."**

This saying echoes the previous saying.

The "living one in your presence" is what truly speaks and acts, the Radiant Presence. This "living one" is not recognized by world views that hold actions to be performed by autonomously existing beings who are independent doers. Radiant Presence alone "lives"; apparent entities ("twenty-four prophets") have no autonomous existence, but are imaginary subdivisions of the Radiance defined into existence in imagination, whereas only the Radiance has actual existence.

The "twenty-four prophets" are the "dead," since as separate beings, and stories of history, they are imaginary abstractions, empty forms (the "dead"), being in actuality the Radiance only.

(56) Jesus said this:

"Whoever has come to understand the world has found a corpse, and whoever has found a corpse is superior to the world."

This saying echoes the previous two.

If the yogi comes to "understand the world," they will see that all the supposed things, entities, and conditions that supposedly make up the "world" are actually imaginary definitions being applied to apparent patternings that the Radiance appears as. They have no life in themselves, so are like empty forms, "corpse(s)."

The inherent intelligence that alone has the ability to know this ("whoever has found a corpse") is actually the Radiant Presence itself, which is "superior" to the imaginary conditions of the world, being actual and supreme.

(59) Jesus said,
"Orient to the living one while you are alive,
lest you die and seek to see him and be unable to do so."

This saying urges the yogi to investigate their experience while they are able in order to fully recognize the Radiant Presence (the "living one"), since conditions may change, making Yoga more difficult, due to actual death or the metaphorical death of being lost in identifying with a "dead" orientation (believing in imaginary interpretations that hinder recognition of the Radiance).

(66) Jesus said,
"Show me the stone which the builders have rejected.
That one is the cornerstone."

This saying indicates the way that people who are lost in fantasy, orienting to an interpreted version of a world, do not give value to the actuality of experiencing, Radiant Presence. They are concerned only with the apparent things and situations that they *think* they are experiencing, which are ideas in imagination. Experiencing itself is the "stone" that is "rejected," in placing value only in what appears and not how it is appearing.

But they have everything backwards — experiencing itself is Radiant Presence, the only important thing (hence "cornerstone"), which they hold as valueless ("have rejected"). The things and situations that they value are mere fantasies. Thus the fact that experiencing is Radiant Presence is the basis, the "cornerstone," for understanding reality.

> **(77) Jesus said,**
> **"I am the light which is above everything.**
> **I am the all. From me did everything come forth,**
> **and everything dissolves in me.**
> **Split a piece of wood, and I am there.**
> **Lift up the stone, and you will find me there."**

This saying encapsulates Radiant Presence.

In saying, "I am the light which is above everything," Jesus identifies himself with the Radiance ("light"), which is "above" (prior to) all apparitions ("everything").

In saying, "I am the all. From me did everything come forth, and everything dissolves in me," he identifies himself to be the Radiance (which is what everything is, the "all"). Anything that seems to come into being or to disappear is merely the dynamism of the apparition of this ("From me did everything come forth").

As Radiant Presence is everywhere (or more precisely "everywhere" is in It), then naturally his examples of the wood and the stone are literally true.

An important aspect of this saying is the clarity of Jesus identifying himself specifically to be the Radiance ("I am the light which is above everything"). There is no separate individual, and the realized yogi discovers themself to be nothing other than the Radiance entirely, inclusive of the apparent body, personality structure, apparent thoughts and motivations, etc.

(83) Jesus said this:
"The images are manifest to man, but the light which is in them is hidden in the image of the light of the Father.
He will be revealed, and his image concealed by his light."

The "images" which are "manifest to man" are the interpreted objects, entities, and circumstances that make up the seeming world of the individual from a human perspective.

"The light which is in them" is the Radiance they actually consist of, which is "hidden" in the uninterpretable apparent patterning that the experiential field presents as ("image of the light"). It is "hidden" because what it is in itself is unresolvable, and not obvious to superficial interpretation.

The "image" is "of the Light of the Father," since the shining forth of the experiential qualities and textures of the Radiance ("image of the light") is done by the inherent creative nature of Radiant Presence (the "Father").

The Radiance is experienced as the infinite experiential differentiation of experience, but exactly what it is can never be defined or pinned down, so remains "hidden" even though its apparent patterning is being experienced.

This saying may be confusing since the same word "image(s)" is used in two senses: first ("images") to indicate the apparently coherent entities, objects, and conditions that interpretation claims to resolve apparition into, and secondly ("image") as the uninterpretable apparent patterning of the infinitely differentiation of the Radiance itself.

The last sentence elaborates on the second half of the first sentence; that Radiant Presence ("he") is revealed by the Presence of experience, but exactly what it is ("his image") is unresolvable ("concealed") due to the infinite and unresolvable nature of the Radiance ("by his light").

(84) Jesus said,
"When you see your likeness, you rejoice.
But when you see the images of your origin,
which neither die nor shine forth,
how much will you understand?"

The first sentence of this saying refers to the eager investment ("you rejoice") of one lost in the human perspective, in the intricacies of their interpreted version of their circumstances, their "vision" of things ("your likeness").

But when the raw, infinite differentiation of the Radiance, origin and matrix of "all things," is seen as it is ("see the images of your origin"), which has no cessation or beginning ("which neither die nor shine forth"), can it be understood from within an interpreted perspective? It is impossible to "understand" the Radiance as it is except within its own irrational, transcendental perspective, beyond the context of any interpretation, and here Jesus wonders how much the disciples will rise to the occasion.

(87) Jesus said,

"Wretched is the body that clings to being a body, and wretched is the soul that clings to these two."

The first "body" is the actual unresolvable Radiant experiential qualities that are the basis of being thought of as a body. If that is defined in imagination to actually BE the conceptually defined body, being "clung to (as) being a body", existing materially and independently, this would be "wretched."

The "soul" is the all-present experiencing intelligence of Radiant Presence, which in orienting to being a body in this way ("clings to these two") minimizes its appreciation of its true transcendental nature, entirely beyond yet inclusive of all form; hence it is "wretched."

(89) Jesus said,
"Why do you wash the outside of the cup?
Do you not realize that he who created the inside
is also he who made the outside?"

This saying admonishes the yogi against trying to purify or improve ("wash") their seemingly outer conditions ("outside of the cup") of behavior, personality, social status, body, etc.

This is unnecessary since the primal, creative, absolute purity of Radiant Presence ("he who created the inside is also he who made the outside"), the substance and origin of all, fully applies not only to the purity of consciousness (the "inside") but also to all apparitions (the "outside"). All of these are nothing other than transcendentally pure, apparent patternings of the Radiance as well, and hence unimprovable.

**(91) They said to him,
"Tell us who you are so that we may believe in you."
He said to them, "You read the face of the sky and of the earth,
but you have not recognized the one who is before you,
and you do not know how to read this moment."**

Here the disciples want Jesus to clearly tell them who/what he is.

In answer, he criticizes that they are aware only of the superficial aspects of their experience ("you read the face of the sky and of the earth"), the "face" of things. Thus they "have not recognized" the actual nature of the experiential field ("the one who is before you"), the revelation of Radiant Presence; and they do not see ("do not know how to read") that this is the entirety that exists "now" ("this moment"), the actuality of this right here, right now: Radiant Presence.

(94) Jesus said,
"He who seeks will find, and he who knocks will be let in."

Jesus assures the yogi that if he investigate his experience sensitively and with intelligence, he will be able to discover its nature ("he who seeks will find").

Further, anyone who sincerely inquires of someone who knows this condition will receive assistance in coming to understand this nature ("he who knocks will be let in").

> **(99)** The disciples said to him,
> "Your brothers and your mother are standing outside."
> He said to them,
> "Those here who do the will of my Father are
> my brothers and my mother.
> It is they who will enter the Kingdom of my Father."

Here the disciples refer to Jesus' human relatives. Jesus corrects them, telling them in effect to not orient to human relations, saying that the only important relationships are with fellow yogis who are oriented to knowing the Radiance ("those here who do the will of my Father").

They, being oriented to the Radiance ("do the will of my Father"), will discover that they are one with the true condition ("enter the Kingdom").

(106) Jesus said,
"When you make the two one, you will become the sons of man, and when you say, 'Mountain, move away,' it will move away."

To "make the two one" is to orient to the experiential field as the single, infinite, inclusive continuum that it actually is. The "two" are all dichotomies; for example: subject and object, self and other, here and there, this and that, etc. In doing this, one realizes the actual condition (the experiential field, the field of Radiant Presence) which is undivided, even though infinitely differentiated in terms of the apparent qualities of its apparition.

"Become sons of man" refers to realizing that they are virtual subsystems of, and within, the Radiance. They are referred to as sons of Adam, who being directly created by God exists explicitly in the pure direct relationship of all apparition to Radiant Presence; and being his "son" means to live in a similar oneness within the Radiance as Adam.

Then being one with Radiant Presence, the cause of all apparent phenomena, you are that cause, and hence all phenomena appear and move in accordance with your actual will.

**(108) Jesus said,
"He who will drink from my mouth will become like me.
I myself shall become he, and what is hidden will be
revealed to him."**

Here the true spiritual relationship is revealed.

When the disciple truly sees what the master is teaching ("drinks from my mouth"), they realize the true condition that they are, and that they are in the same state as the master ("will become like me"). This is realization.

Since the Radiant Presence that the disciple discovers themself to be is ultimately the same Radiant Presence that the master is, then what the master is becomes explicitly what the disciple is ("I myself shall become he").

In a more esoteric sense, this mystery of "transmission" is that a profound, psychic, resonant identity is established between master and disciple ("I myself shall become he"), enabling the fullness of realization through sharing psychically, absolutely intimately, the direct experience of the Radiance. This has been called "sharing the mind outside the teaching" in early Buddhism.

As the disciple shares the point of view of the master, what had been hidden from the student that the master knows becomes revealed ("what is hidden will be revealed to him").

**(113) His disciples said to him, "When will the Kingdom come?"
Jesus said, "It will not come by waiting for it.
It will not be a matter of saying 'here it is' or 'there it is.'
Rather, the Kingdom of the Father is spread out upon the earth,
and men do not see it."**

The disciples inquire when the true condition will appear, "the Kingdom come."

In saying "It will not come by waiting for it," they are told it is not related to time. Then they are told it is not related to space, being neither "here" nor "there."

The true condition, Radiant Presence (the "Kingdom"), is everywhere that there is experiential appearance ("is spread out upon the earth"), but it is not recognized as it is due to the misinterpretation of the human perspective ("and men do not see it").

AFTERWORD

The lucid directions of Jesus presented here are eternally true and valid, as much so now as they were two thousand years ago.

That the nature of what this is, what YOU are, is both so available to discover, and so astounding and magnificent, is truly the "good news" that the word *gospel* promises, and that this book fully lives up to.

The true promise of Christianity, the blessing of the Christ, is here given generously and completely. I find it sad that orthodox Christianity did not include this empowerment in its official canon. We are indeed fortunate that it was discovered within the scrolls recovered at Nag Hammadi, and so is available to those whose fortune it is to come upon it.

May all benefit from this Truth.

Peter Brown
Sausalito, CA
August, 2020

theopendoorway.org

Also by Peter Brown

Dirty Enlightenment

Essence of Recognition

The Yoga of Radiant Presence

Printed in Great Britain
by Amazon